PIGS & PORK
in the story of agriculture

Susan Anderson and JoAnne Buggey

Book design by Nancy Roberts

Northwest Arm Press

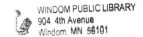

Hello!

I'm Agri-Culture, Agri for short.

I'm here to introduce **pigs and pork**, an important agricultural product.

We will see pigs and pork in all five parts of agriculture:

production > processing > distribution > marketing > consumerism

Let's go!

Chapter 1 • The **production** of pigs

Agricultural production is growing crops or raising animals.

| production | processing | distribution | marketing | consumerism |

- farms
- care of pigs
- nutrient cycle

This is a **farm** where pigs are raised. Crops are grown on this farm to help feed the pigs.

Did you know?

Most pigs eat feed that includes corn, soybeans, and wheat.

It's a fact!

Pigs are not native to North America. The explorer Hernando de Soto is reported to have brought pigs to Florida in 1539. They would have looked quite different from the pigs we see on farms today.

Farmers who raise pigs as a business are pork producers. The meat from pigs is called pork.

Did you know?

Some pork producers manage farms that have been passed down in their family from generation to generation. It is a way of life and a business.

It's a fact!

On many farms caretakers shower and put on clean clothes before entering the barns. Showering prevents germs from being spread to the pigs.

Mother pigs are called **sows.** Newborn pigs are **piglets.** They drink milk from the sow.

It's a fact!

A sow's pregnancy lasts about 112–115 days, about 3½ months. Piglets weigh an average of 2½–4½ pounds at birth.

Did you know?

Other words for pigs: hogs, swine
Boar – a male pig
Gilt – a young female pig who has not given birth
Litter – a group of pigs born at one time

Good feed and **fresh water** are necessary for growing healthy pigs and producing wholesome food products.

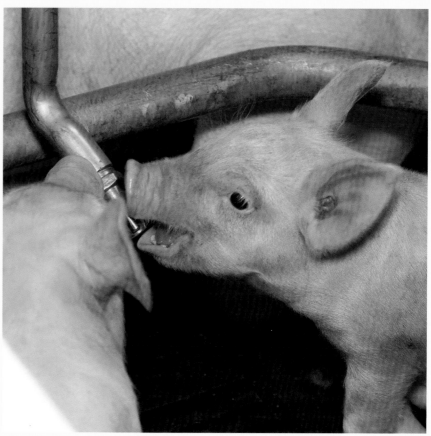

It's a fact!

On some farms sows give birth in farrowing barns. Piglets are moved to a nursery barn at about three weeks old. There they are given solid feed and learn to drink from waterers.

Did you know?

Pigs do not overeat. They eat until they are full. A pig eats about $2\frac{1}{2}$ pounds of feed to gain a pound.

Pork producers carefully control the barn **temperature** to keep pigs healthy and comfortable. Ventilation fans are used in most barns to help maintain good air quality.

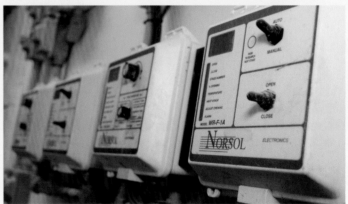

Did you know?

Veterinarians will often visit the barns to observe the health of the pigs.

It's a fact!

Pigs cannot sweat, so on hot summer days the animals may be sprinkled by water misters to keep them cool. In winter pork producers might use heat lamps to keep the pigs warm.

Pork producers want pigs that provide **lean** meat. Most of today's lean and fast-growing market pigs combine the best qualities of the four important **breeds** on this page.

Did you know?

Today's pork producers raise pigs that are much leaner than this prize-winning 4-H-raised pig of the 1920s.

Landrace

Yorkshire

Duroc

Hampshire

It's a fact!

Some pigs have ears that stand up. Others have floppy ears.

Pig waste, called manure, is valuable. It is used in a fertilizing system called the **nutrient cycle.**

Did you know?

- Pigs make manure.

- Farmers store it.

- Later it is spread on fields to fertilize crops.

- Some of the crops become feed for more pigs ...

  and the cycle starts over!

It's a fact!

As a fertilizer, manure provides important nutrients. They include nitrogen, phosphorous, and potassium, which are essential for growing crops.

MANURE STORAGE

Chapter 2 • The **processing** of pork

Processing is making crops or animals into products you can eat or use.

production	**processing**	distribution	marketing	consumerism

- meat
- by-products

In a **processing plant** meat is prepared from animals – pigs become pork.

It's a fact!

Pork is one of the world's most widely eaten meats.

Did you know?

Keeping food safe to eat is a top priority. Government agencies create and enforce rules that make the meat industry one of the most regulated and inspected.

U.S. INSPECTED AND PASSED BY DEPARTMENT OF AGRICULTURE EST. 791

A pork processing plant can produce many kinds of pork products.
One of the first products is **fresh pork.**

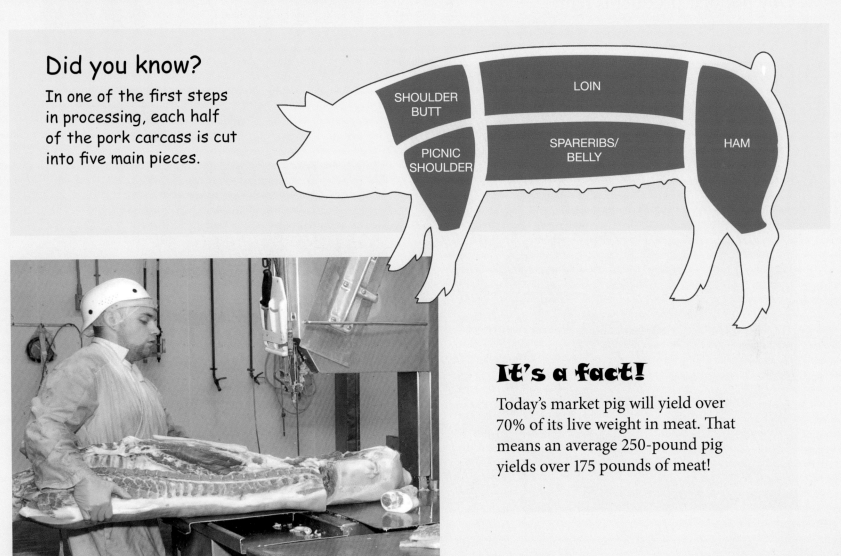

Did you know?

In one of the first steps in processing, each half of the pork carcass is cut into five main pieces.

SHOULDER BUTT

LOIN

PICNIC SHOULDER

SPARERIBS/ BELLY

HAM

It's a fact!

Today's market pig will yield over 70% of its live weight in meat. That means an average 250-pound pig yields over 175 pounds of meat!

Some pork is **further processed.** Fresh pork might be partially cooked and smoked with seasonings added. One popular product is ham.

It's a fact!

Bacon was one of the first foods eaten by astronauts on the moon.

Did you know?
Bacon is the pork belly smoked and thinly sliced.

Other pork products go through many steps in processing. They are considered **fully processed.** They still need to be kept refrigerated in the store and at home.

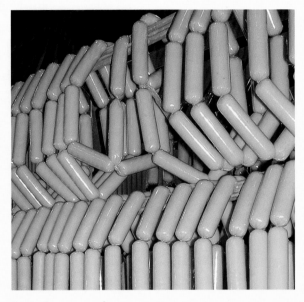

Did you know?
Sausages and wieners are sometimes called links because they are linked together when they are being made.

It's a fact!
Some sausages start out 10 feet long. The tube is stuffed with a meat-and-seasonings mixture, and then the sausages are cooked.

Canned pork products are found in the non-refrigerated area of the grocery store and can be eaten without further cooking.

It's a fact!
There is a SPAM® Museum!

Did you know?
Pork canning started in the 1860s. Today canned pork products include spreads, lunch meat, and sausages.

Many **by-products** are produced in the processing of pork. Some of these by-products are used in other foods.

Did you know?

Gelatin is a by-product made from pigs. Gelatin is used as a thickener in many food products.

It's a fact!

Marshmallows are mostly sugars and whipped-up gelatin.

Non-food items also contain by-products of pork processing.

Did you know?

It is often said that pork processing uses everything but the OINK! A researcher who followed one pig from processing onward found that a piece or substance from that pig ended up in 184 different products.

It's a fact!

Pig bladders are used as tambourine heads. Pig hair makes the bristles in many brushes.

Chapter 3 • The **distribution** of pork

Distribution is delivering a product from where it is produced or processed to the places where it will be used.

production ▸ processing ▸ **distribution** ▸ marketing ▸ consumerism ▸

- pork-producing states
- transportation
- U.S. pork exports

Pigs are raised throughout the **United States.**

Did you know?

Pigs are raised in every state. The top 3 and the top 10 pig-raising states are shown in color.

It's a fact!

Pigs are often raised in areas where corn, soybeans, and wheat are grown.

After processing, pork products have to be **transported** to stores or distribution centers.

It's a fact!

Refrigerated transportation is very important to the pork industry.

Did you know?

Pork producers take pride in their ability to provide quality foods for consumers throughout the United States and around the world.

Pork is a leading United States **export.** When fresh or frozen pork products are shipped around the world, they must be carried in refrigerated containers or holds.

Did you know?

China produces more pork than any other country, but it also imports pork from the United States. Half of all U.S. pork exports go to Asian countries.

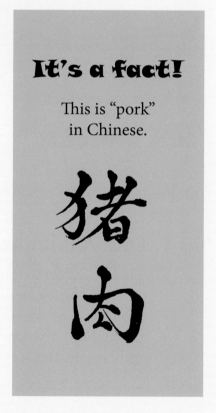

It's a fact!

This is "pork" in Chinese.

猪肉

Chapter 4 • The marketing of pork

Marketing is telling about products so that you will know about them and might buy them.

| production | processing | distribution | **marketing** | consumerism |

- advertising
- pork promotional items
- expos, meetings, and fairs

Advertising tells us how good it is to eat pork.

U.S. PORK

Did you know?

Advertising tries to persuade you to buy or use a product or service. Some of the places you might see or hear about pork and pork products include television, radio, magazines, newspapers, and the Internet.

INDIANA PORK

Specials

Pork Ribs
1, 2, or 3 racks in
own sticky BBQ

Pulled pork
piled high with
tenderest pork

It's a fact!

Pork advertising has catchy slogans.

The Other White Meat

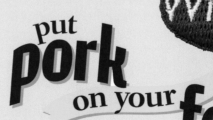

put **pork** on your **fork**

We are **influenced** to buy products in many ways.

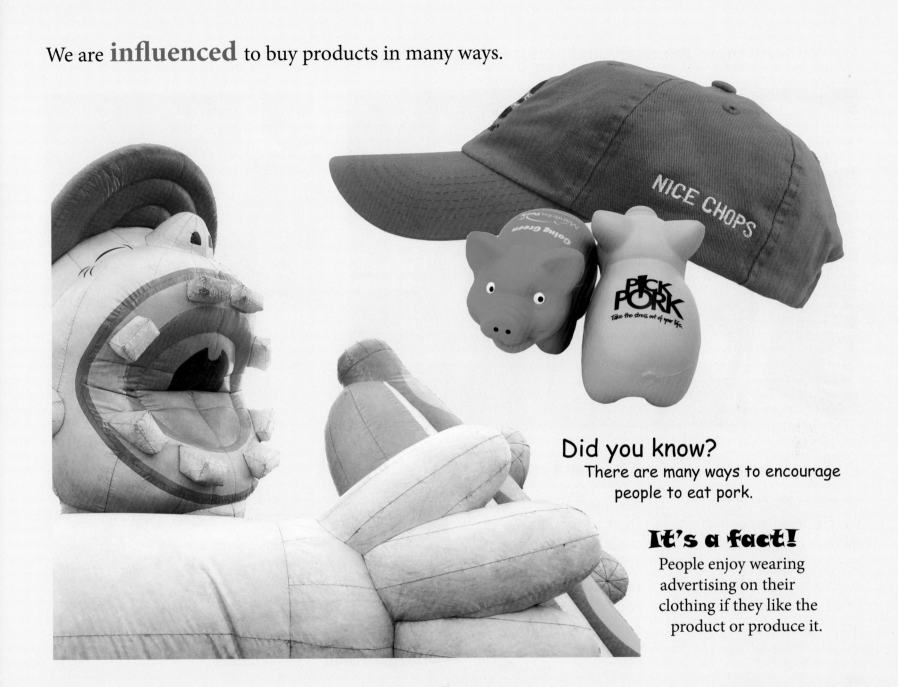

NICE CHOPS

Going Green

PICK PORK
Take the stress out of your life.

Did you know?
There are many ways to encourage
people to eat pork.

It's a fact!
People enjoy wearing
advertising on their
clothing if they like the
product or produce it.

We can learn more about pigs and pork products at **expos and fairs.**

Did you know?

World Pork Expo meets yearly. People come from all over the world. This meeting shows the latest technology and products. Producers examine important issues.

It's a fact!

4-H members may share information about their pig projects at fairs. Young people can receive trophies and ribbons for raising quality pigs.

Chapter 5 • Consumerism and pork

Consumerism is **you** choosing, buying, and using products.

production ▸ processing ▸ distribution ▸ marketing ▸ **consumerism**

- MyPyramid
- buying and cooking pork
- pork dishes
- pigskin products

Pork is in the **Meat & Beans** group.

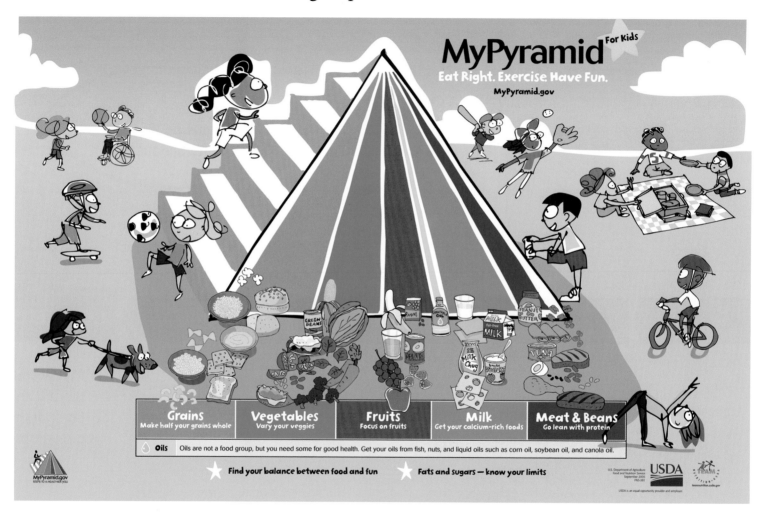

Did you know?

You should eat two servings from Meat & Beans every day. A serving of pork is about the size of a computer mouse.

It's a fact!

Pork is a good source of protein, vitamins, and minerals. Thiamine, niacin, riboflavin, vitamin B_6, phosphorous, zinc, iron, potassium – these nutrients make pork a wholesome, healthy food.

The **grocery store** offers a large number of pork products.

Did you know?

Pork chops are the most popular cut of pork.

It's a fact!

The consumption of pork in the United States is around 50 pounds per person per year.

When cooking meat such as pork be sure to **wash** your hands and utensils.

SAFE HANDLING INSTRUCTIONS
THIS PRODUCT WAS PREPARED FROM INSPECTED AND PASSED MEAT AND/OR POULTRY. SOME FOOD PRODUCTS MAY CONTAIN BACTERIA THAT COULD CAUSE ILLNESS IF THE PRODUCT IS MISHANDLED OR COOKED IMPROPERLY. FOR YOUR PROTECTION, FOLLOW THESE SAFE HANDLING INSTRUCTIONS.

KEEP REFRIGERATED OR FROZEN. THAW IN REFRIGERATOR OR MICROWAVE.

KEEP RAW MEAT AND POULTRY SEPARATE FROM OTHER FOODS. WASH WORKING SURFACES (INCLUDING CUTTING BOARDS), UTENSILS, AND HANDS AFTER TOUCHING RAW MEAT OR POULTRY.

COOK THOROUGHLY.

KEEP HOT FOODS HOT. REFRIGERATE LEFTOVERS IMMEDIATELY OR DISCARD.

Did you know?

Pork and other perishable products are dated so you can be sure what you are buying is fresh. When buying pork at the grocery store, always check the expiration date.

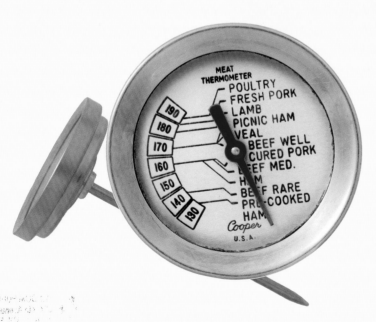

It's a fact!

For a safe and tasty meal, it is important to follow the cooking directions on pork products. Some need to be cooked to a certain temperature, and some are ready to eat.

These are some of the ways **pork products** are eaten.
Point to any you have tried or seen.

Did you know?

There is no ham in a
hamburger – it's all beef –
but you can use ground pork
to make a pork burger.

It's a fact!

One of the top 10 sandwiches
served at home for lunch is a ham
sandwich.

Pigskin is used in many everyday products.

Did you know?
Pig skins are made into leather by a chemical process called tanning.

It's a fact!
Dried pigskin makes a great chew toy for dogs. Footballs are sometimes called "pigskins" because that is what the early ones were made of.

Pigs and pork are an important part of our lives. Maybe **you** will play a role in the future of pigs and pork.

Pig and Pork Activities

Here are the names and shapes of the 10 states that raise the most pigs. Can you match each name with the right shape? You can check your answers on page 20.

Illinois
Indiana
Iowa
Kansas
Minnesota
Missouri
Nebraska
North Carolina
Ohio
Oklahoma

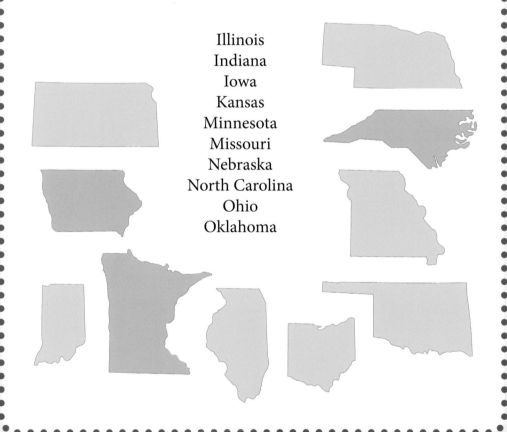

Write your own story about each chapter.

In your grocery store find examples of fresh, processed, and canned pork.

Divide a piece of paper into four parts and draw a picture in each part about pigs or pork.

Write a poem or rap about pigs or pork.

Go to the website www.pork4kids.com. Try one activity.

More titles in
The Story of Agriculture series

Soybeans in the Story of Agriculture
American Farm Bureau Federation 2010 Book of the Year

Pigs & Pork in the Story of Agriculture

forthcoming topics:
 Corn
 Beef
 Wheat
 Dairy
 Poultry

For children ages 5–8, see the
Awesome Agriculture A-to-Z series:

Soybeans, an A-to-Z book
American Farm Bureau Federation
2010 preK– K Accurate Ag Book

Pigs, an A-to-Z book

forthcoming topics:
 Corn
 Beef
 Wheat
 Dairy
 Poultry

Both soybean books are Illinois Ag in the Classroom 2010 Ag Week Books of the Year. *Soybeans in the Story of Agriculture* is also Minnesota Farm Bureau 2010 Book of the Year.

The Authors

JoAnne Buggey has a PhD in Curriculum & Instruction from the University of Washington (1971). She taught future elementary teachers in the College of Education and Human Development at the University of Minnesota. JoAnne has written dozens of textbooks for children, including an American history text, *America! America!* and a civics text, *Civics for Americans.* Her recent multimedia projects include *Exploring Where and Why,* a program on maps and mapping for grades K–3.

Susan Anderson earned her MS in Curriculum & Instruction from Minnesota State University, Mankato (1988). She is an Education Specialist for University of Minnesota Extension in the College of Food, Agricultural and Natural Resource Sciences. Susan grew up on a farm and lives on a working farm today. During her elementary teaching years, she developed an interdisciplinary fifth-grade curriculum to increase agricultural literacy.

Both authors have been elementary teachers in the Minneapolis Public Schools. They currently work with the K–12 Education Program at the University of Minnesota Southwest Research and Outreach Center at Lamberton. They provide workshops for future and current elementary teachers in agricultural literacy. Both have contributed to curriculum projects, including materials related to dairy and pigs. The authors serve on various boards related to agriculture and have won awards for quality teaching about agriculture. JoAnne and Susan are currently part of an Improving Teacher Quality grant team.

Acknowledgements

For invaluable assistance, our thanks go to Lynnelle Mays and Florida 4-H; Carol Banks; Kelly Daynard and the Ontario Farm Animal Council; Clint Schwab, Steve Weintraut, and the National Swine Registry; Dan MacGillivray, Doug McEachern, and the employees of Tony's Meats; Nancy Hill; Gerald and Debbie Vermeulen; Claudia and José van Vilsteren; George Chater and Chater's Meat Market; Jan Jorgensen and Beth Wonderlin, National Pork Board; Kelly Funke, Manitoba Pork Council; Roy Kruse, Alberta Pork; Sarah Ford, Indiana Pork.

• •

This book is dedicated to Bob

• •

Tractor illustrations by Gerry Cleary,
from an original idea by James Jahoda

Northwest Arm Press, Inc.
1004-1545 South Park Street
Halifax Nova Scotia Canada B3J 4B3

Fact-checker: Paddy Muir
Project photographer: Lisa Marie Noseworthy, LMNO Photo
Project illustrator: Gerry Cleary
Copy editor: Jane Fielding Bell
Special thanks to Trudy Wastweet, Minnesota Pork Producers Association

Models:
  5: José and Claudia van Vilsteren, Gerald Vermeulen
  8: Carolyn Smedley
  12: Doug McEachern
  12: Nancy Roberts
  13: Rane O'neil
  15: Stefan Bjornson, Greg Deyoung
  29: Leo Zinati
  32: Lisa Marie Noseworthy
  33: Nancy Roberts, Carolyn Smedley, José and Claudia van Vilsteren, Leo Zinati

Printed by Friesens Corp., Altona, Manitoba, Canada

Library and Archives Canada Cataloguing in Publication

Anderson, Susan, 1950-
    Pigs & pork in the story of agriculture / Susan
Anderson, JoAnne Buggey.

ISBN 978-1-926781-01-3

    1. Swine--Juvenile literature. 2. Pork--Juvenile
literature. I. Buggey, JoAnne II. Title. III. Title: Pigs
and pork in the story of agriculture.

SF395.5.A543 2010   j636.4   C2009-907352-8

Image Credits

Front cover: LMNO Photo
4: main photos, National Pork Board (NPB); in circle, LMNO
    Photo
5: left and right, LMNO Photo; center, Ontario Farm Animal
    Council (OFAC)
6: © Milos Jokic, used under license from Shutterstock.com
7–8: LMNO Photo
9: breeds courtesy of National Swine Registry (NSR); 1920
    courtesy of University of Florida; large pig, Carol Banks
10: illustration by Gerry Cleary
12: LMNO Photo; seal, Nancy Hill
13: illustration courtesy of NPB; LMNO Photo
14: ham © robootb, used under license from Shutterstock.com;
    astronaut, JSC scan courtesy of the National Aeronautics
    and Space Administration; bacon, LMNO Photo
15: left, LMNO Photo; right © Moiseeva Galina Gavrilovna, used
    under license from Shutterstock.com
16: museum, JoAnne Buggey; meats, LMNO Photo.
    SPAM® is a trademark of Hormel Foods, LLC and is being
    used with permission from Hormel Foods. Underwood® is
    a registered trademark of B&G Foods, Inc.
17: LMNO Photo
18: brushes, LMNO Photo; tambourine ©Arturo Limon, used
    under license from Shutterstock.com
20: © Mirec, 2009, used under license from Shutterstock.com
21: LMNO Photo
22: courtesy of NPB; calligraphy, Chai Chu Thompson
24: pig sign, John Driemen; U.S. Pork courtesy of NPB; Indiana
    Pork courtesy of Indiana Pork Producers Association;
    "Put Pork on Your Fork" courtesy of Alberta Pork;
    "The Other White Meat" courtesy of NPB
25: inflatable © Alistair Cotton, used under license from
    Shutterstock.com; hat and pigs, LMNO Photo
26: PigMobile courtesy of OFAC; handshake courtesy of NSR;
    sign, Carol Banks
28: United States Department of Agriculture. USDA does not
    endorse any products, services, or organizations.
29: shopper courtesy of NPB; butcher, LMNO Photo; pork chops
    © Nayashkova Olga, used under license from
    Shutterstock.com
30: labels, Nancy Hill; thermometer, LMNO Photo
31: upper, LMNO Photo; ham © Kelly Cline
32: jacket, gloves, and toy, LMNO Photo; football © Kadroff, used
    under license from Shutterstock.com
33: upper left, courtesy of NSR; remainder, LMNO Photo
Back cover: see credits for pages 6, 10, and 22.

Every effort has been made to credit the copyright holders of the
images reproduced in this book. Any omissions will be rectified
in subsequent printings if notice is given to the publisher.